BENIN EMPIRE

Catherine Chambers

W
FRANKLIN WATTS

First published in 2014 by Franklin Watts

Franklin Watts
338 Euston Road
London NW1 3BH

Franklin Watts Australia
Level 17/207 Kent Street
Sydney, NSW 2000

Editor in Chief: John C. Miles
Editor: Sarah Ridley
Art director: Peter Scoulding
Series designer: John Christopher/White Design
Picture research: Diana Morris

Dewey number: 966

Hardback ISBN 978 1 4451 3418 5
Library eBook ISBN 978 1 44513417 8

Printed in China

Franklin Watts is a division of Hachette Children's Books,
an Hachette UK company.

www.hachette.co.uk

CONTENTS

THE KINGDOM OF BENIN

The Kingdom of Benin was one of West Africa's many great kingdoms and empires and was built by the Edo people. Its political organisation, trading skill, belief system and rich culture are celebrated to this day. People admire the kingdom's artforms created in brass, ivory, terracotta and wood. How and when did it all begin?

How do we know?

The early history of the Edo people between the 9th and 13th centuries is difficult to piece together since they left no written records. However, historians have used archaeological evidence, spoken history and traditions that are still practised today to build a picture of when and how the civilisation began.

A kingdom in the forest

It is hard to imagine how, more than 1,000 years ago, a vast, wealthy kingdom emerged and grew deep inside sub-tropical rainforest. Yet this is exactly the setting of the Kingdom of Benin, which was first known as Igodomigodo. Benin's origins lie in what is now south-west Nigeria, close to the Atlantic Ocean. The River Benue lies far to the north-east, while the mighty River Niger streams across the north and down to its east.

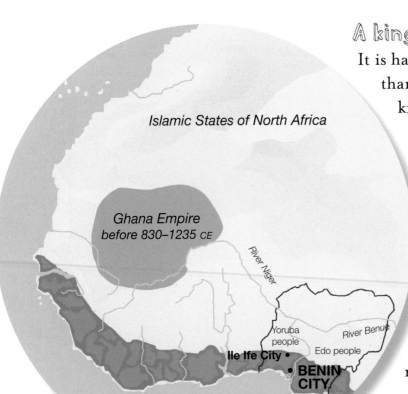

Islamic States of North Africa

Ghana Empire
before 830–1235 CE

River Niger

Yoruba people

River Benue

Edo people

Ile Ife City •

• BENIN CITY

ATLANTIC OCEAN

This map shows West Africa around 900 CE. Modern-day countries in the region include Nigeria, Benin (a country whose name has no connection with Benin City), Ghana, Sierra Leone, Guinea, Gambia and Senegal. The red line shows the border of modern-day Nigeria.

Boats ferry goods and people on the modern-day River Niger. Trading goods along rivers and the coast brought wealth to the Kingdom of Benin.

Moving to the forest

The Edo were not the first people to live in the area but we know they built up the Kingdom of Benin. We also know that they came from further north, probably where the rivers Niger and Benue meet. Here, maybe as much as 6,000 years ago, the Edo grazed animals on open savannah and grassland. We do not know why they had to move south. Maybe other people wanted their grazing land.

The first written records

The artefacts shown in this book date from many centuries after 900 CE. This is because Benin was closed to the world outside Africa until the late 1400s. Then, Portuguese and Dutch ships sailed toward the Niger River Delta and written records of the city and empire began. Unfortunately for Benin, it declined as the Yoruba State around Ile Ife grew. Benin finally lost its independence when British troops attacked and looted the city in 1897. Today Benin City is a bustling city in modern-day Nigeria.

5

INSIDE THE GREAT WALLS

Benin City was at the heart of the kingdom. The city began as a group of scattered villages, each with a chief, whose leaders bowed to the power of central kings called Ogiso. Through trade, Benin City grew wealthy and expanded. In the 13th century new kings, the Oba, took over from the Ogiso. Huge walls and moats were built to surround and protect the city.

Cutting edge

Benin's inner walls were made of clay and wood. The skill of Edo builders allowed them to build these structures to a great height. The outer walls were smaller. One visitor to Benin in the 1600s described them as a double row of tall tree trunks set close together and daubed with thick clay. Benin City in the 1400s was a grand and beautiful place.

This Dutch picture of Benin City was made in the 1600s. The royal palace where the Oba lived is the building with the tall spires. The Oba is shown on horseback in the foreground.

6

The walls around Benin City once measured 1,200 km in length. Only small sections of wall and ditch remain today, as shown here.

More than defences

Benin City's inner walls were defensive, protecting the royal palace. But the outer walls divided the palace, the palace officials' and craftsmen's quarters from the farms outside. Later, in the 15th century, probably under Oba Ewuare the Great, the walls were built up even higher and the great moat, or Iya, dug deeper. Some ramparts reached at least 20 metres in height.

Inside the city

Benin City's walls and the buildings within them were built on a low, sandy, flat area of land covered in subtropical trees and plants. The walls loomed large yet the rectangular buildings inside were single storey. Wide main roads crisscrossed with smaller streets separated the areas where different craftsmen and their families made their homes and workshops. From the 16th century, European traders, ambassadors and travellers were overawed by its size, grandeur and cleanliness.

Around the world

c. 3000–1460 BCE Pakistan/India
So far, we know of over 1,400 towns and cities from the Indus Valley Civilisation. The great cities of Harappa and Mohenjo-Daro were designed on a grid system.

c. 3000–30 BCE Egypt
New technology is uncovering more about Egypt's past, disclosing hundreds of previously undiscovered buildings and boundary walls buried in the sand.

c. 2000 BCE–900 CE Central America
The Maya build huge unplanned cities. The city of Tikal has over 10,000 buildings. Some are large stone palaces built around grand squares. Others are small thatched houses.

DIVINE HEAD

The Oba ruled over the Kingdom of Benin as its spiritual and political leader. He controlled all trade between the kingdom and outsiders. The way he dressed — his headdress and his neck rings — set him apart from his people. He was treated like a god, and he expected this.

The power of mystery

The Oba's people believed that he came from an unbroken line of rulers that went all the way back to the son of the Supreme God, Osanobua. The Oba shrouded himself in mystery and magic. Most of the time he saw only protective palace officials, his wives, doctors, servants and priests.

The cradle of the world

Benin's traditional creation story tells how the Supreme God, Osanobua, sent his children to Earth, which at that time was just water and air. But the youngest took a shell and when he reached Earth he tipped it upside down. Sand flowed from the shell, creating dry land – Benin – and the youngest child became the first king. All Ogiso and Oba are linked to him.

This brass metal head of an Oba dates from the 1700s CE. It was placed on an altar for future Obas to honour.

Skilled craftsmen continue to work in Benin City, Nigeria, today. Brass casting methods here have not changed in hundreds of years.

Royal craftsmen

The Oba gathered a community of highly skilled craftspeople around him. They lived in the palace and spent their lives making brass, ivory and wood sculptures for the Oba, his chiefs and priests. The brass or bronze — a mixture of copper and zinc or tin — was used to make objects made using the lost wax process. This involved making a wax model first, which melted, leaving a hollow clay mould that was filled with molten brass.

Around the world

c. 3000–1460 BCE Pakistan/India
Copper and brass artefacts including tools have been found in Indus Valley Civilisation cities such as Harappa. Metalworkers smelt the metal in large clay pots called crucibles.

• •

c. 3000–30 BCE Egypt
Egyptian craftsmen work first with copper, then with bronze, using the lost wax process. Some works are created in parts and then joined together.

• •

c. 1600–1460 BCE China
During the Shang Dynasty, bronze casters use the piece-mould method. Clay is wrapped around a carved model of the object, is cut away in sections and then put together after firing. The clay mould is filled with liquid bronze.

• •

INSIDE THE PALACE

The Oba lived in a grand palace. Inside, he consulted with the Uzama, a high council of chiefs. This ancient body of elders is thought to have been created by Ogiso Eweka I in the early 1200s CE. The Uzama was just one part of a complex government and society.

There is still an Oba and a palace in Benin City. The modern palace has a large central courtyard with many rooms leading off it.

10

Moving house

There was often trouble between the Ogiso king and the Uzama. This was because the chiefs who formed the Uzama did not owe their positions to him. The first Oba, Ewedo, took over from the Ogiso in about 1255. He was determined to curb the Uzama's power. So he moved his palace, which was in the middle of the Uzama chiefs' villages, to the centre of Benin City. From here, he developed his image as an all-powerful king.

This picture of the late Oba Akenzua II was taken in 1964 and shows his elaborate coral garment and headpiece.

11

Cutting edge

Each village was led by an Odionwere – the oldest man. Together, these village heads formed a ruling council, which in turn was led by the oldest man, the Oka Edionwere. But he was often frail and not always wise. So the next oldest, the Okaiko, often helped him. One Okaiko, called Igodo, rose above them all and established the first dynasty of Benin kings, the Ogiso. Oral tradition says this was way back in 40 BCE, although most historians place it much later.

Knowing your place

Everyone knew their place in Benin society. Within clans and villages, each person belonged to an age grade in which they carried out certain duties and learned skills. After some years, they moved up to the next grade. As for the Ogiso and Oba, they devised laws, made war and prevented disease, with the help of advisors.

Around the world

c. 3000–30 BCE Egypt
Egyptians believe that the heavenly gods rule them. The pharaohs are seen as gods, too. They control all aspects of life and are assisted by viziers.

1600 to 1050 BCE China
The king and noble families rule from the Shang capital city near Anyang. Shang Dynasty kings often quarrel with nobles.

c. 900 CE Middle East
The Caliph rules from the Persian city of Baghdad. He is a religious leader as well as a political leader, and is helped by viziers, or advisors.

FEARSOME WARRIORS

Benin was not always a peaceful kingdom so the king, or Oba, had a large army with plenty of weapons. The Ogiso, and later, the Oba, often had their power challenged by chiefs within the kingdom. Benin also needed to protect its trade routes and borders from outsiders.

12

A ceremonial sword from the Oba's palace, inside a scabbard made of coral beads. The Oba is often shown holding a sword like this.

Weapons of war

The king could call on thousands of soldiers to help him. They were equipped with curved iron swords and knives, and harpoon-like spears. They carried bows that fired poison-tipped arrows. Soldiers wore armour made of thick, quilted material covered in leopard skin to repel arrows and sword cuts. Shields were made of wood and animal hides stretched over a basketwork frame. Officers and other senior soldiers wore helmets covered with hardened crocodile skin.

Style and function

The sword shown above was made later than the 13th century but has been made in Benin's classic curved style. The coral beads, too, were a later addition, as coral was not used in this way until the 1400s. However, craftsmen were proud of traditional styles. So early beadwork did exist, only made from other materials such as coloured glass and stone.

This brass statue of a Benin warrior dates from the 1600s CE, but earlier soldiers may have looked the same. Soldiers on horseback guarded the Oba and took part in processions.

Smelting skills

Metalworking at the site of Benin took place hundreds of years before the kingdom emerged. But Benin did not have any iron deposits of its own. These lay far to the north. The inhabitants of Benin knew that it was important to obtain iron to make strong tools and weapons. Before this time, there was only wood, flint and stone. With iron, they developed smelting skills and metal craftsmanship to create strong, elegant weapons.

13

Around the world

c. 4000–2000 BCE Sumer

Over 7,000 years ago, the first people to inhabit Sumer are the Ubaids, who make metal hoes for digging the earth and sickles for harvesting grain.
They also make knives and adzes.

1600-1050 BCE China

Weapons are made from bronze during the Shang Dynasty. Some are weapon heads attached to wooden handles. One of these is the 'ge', which is a type of spiked axe. Some soldiers ride on horseback while others charge around in chariots.

c. 900 CE Middle East

The Abbasid rulers of the Persian city of Baghdad have great armies. They guard the river that runs through the city in case invaders sail in. Soldiers parade around the grand square in front of the ruler's palace.

A LAND OF PLENTY

Benin's wide range of iron tools enabled farmers to hunt, fish and grow plenty of food crops. Clearings in the forest provided light for the plants. The soils were good, the weather was warm and water was abundant. The people of Benin ate well and had a varied diet.

14

Eating well

The Edo kept chickens, goats and cattle, although the cows' milk was not drunk. The tastiest meats were supplied by forest hunters, who were highly skilled and had excellent weapons. The hunters' prey included antelopes, grasscutter rats, pangolins – a tree-dwelling anteater – dwarf crocodiles and red river hogs. The streams and creeks were full of seafood and fish, like the mudfish in the picture.

This stool dates from between the 1500s–1700s CE. It is cast in the shape of two large, wriggling mudfish – a fisherman's favourite, a tasty catch and an Edo symbol of plenty.

Yams for sale in a West African market. At harvest time - roughly the beginning of August – the New Yam festival took place, as it does today.

Crop control

Benin's kings had a firm control over farming. Yams were an important crop because they are a high-energy food and store well. But harvesting them required a lot of labour, so the kings used slaves as well as local farmworkers. Yam growing needed so many slaves that, for a long time, the Obas were reluctant to sell male slaves to European traders.

Wonderful water

When Europeans came to the Kingdom of Benin they were surprised to find that the Edo used ancient skills to keep water fresh. Water was stored in enormous clay pots, which kept it cool. Medicinal herbs from the forest stopped the water from going stagnant and smelly. These water pots were placed at the main markets and trading posts throughout the kingdom. European merchants brought back tales of the guards, who made sure that anyone wanting drinking water paid for it!

Around the world

**c. 3000-1500 BCE
Pakistan/India**
People irrigate their crops from rivers close to their towns and cities. Rivers also provided plenty of fish.

c. 3000–30 BCE Egypt
The River Nile brings fertility and water to farmers' fields. Hunters kill fish, birds, crocodile and hippos for their meat.

**c. 2000 BCE–900 CE
Central America**
On the lowlands, the Maya grow maize and manioc as well as squash, beans, chilli peppers and amaranth.

TRADE GOODS AND GREAT KINGDOMS

The main picture below shows a stylishly carved wooden box in the shape of a cow's head. The box is made very skilfully but the most important thing is its contents, which were kola nuts — a stimulant that helps to keep you awake. These nuts and other trade goods helped turn a cluster of small villages into a great trading nation.

16

Chiefs offered the Oba kola nuts from containers like this carved wooden cow's head. It is decorated with copper and brass strips.

Profit and power

Benin's forests were rich in desirable goods such as spices, raffia to make cloth, and elephants' ivory. For hundreds of years before the kingdom arose, villages were trading these goods within West Africa and beyond. Profitable trade required organisation, which was more efficient if the villagers worked together. It also required clever merchants and skilful leaders. So it is thought that the first trade links within West Africa sparked the birth of the Kingdom of Benin.

Cutting edge

Early Edo traders carried trade goods on their heads along forest footpaths to nearby peoples and kingdoms. This meant that the goods needed to be lightweight. The horse, so often depicted, could not travel far, so was not used as a pack animal. This was due partly to the thick forest but more to the tsetse fly, whose bite gave horses *nagana*, a deadly disease.

17

Many materials

Benin's craftsmen used a wide range of fine metal tools made by the kingdom's ironworkers. Woodworkers from the carpenters' guild, the Onwina, hewed out wooden plates, bowls and pestles and mortars with them. Ivory workers from the Igbesanmwan guild carved intricately patterned bracelets and ivory tusks. Later, they made goods such as salt cellars, which the Obas gave to or traded with European merchants.

This picture shows ebony trees in a Nigerian forest. Ebony is very hard, strong and resistant to termites. Benin's skilled woodworkers produced many different objects from ebony, which has a glossy black finish when carved and polished.

Around the world

3000-1500 BCE Pakistan/India
Boats carry trade goods along rivers. On land, goods are carried in carts pulled by bullocks.

1600-1050 BCE China
The Shang Dynasty is mostly located around the Yangtze River. Merchants trade with nearby Japan, Taiwan and Korea.

c. 900 CE Middle East
Islamic rulers control trade networks running from China to Africa and Europe. Trading ships carry goods across the Red Sea while camel trains cross deserts.

MONEY MATTERS

The stunning brass bracelet shown below was worn by royalty and the wealthy. But brass bracelets had another function. In their plain, undecorated form, they were used as a form of money called a manilla. 'Manilla' is actually a Portuguese word meaning 'bracelet' but manillas were used long before European traders reached West Africa's shores.

18

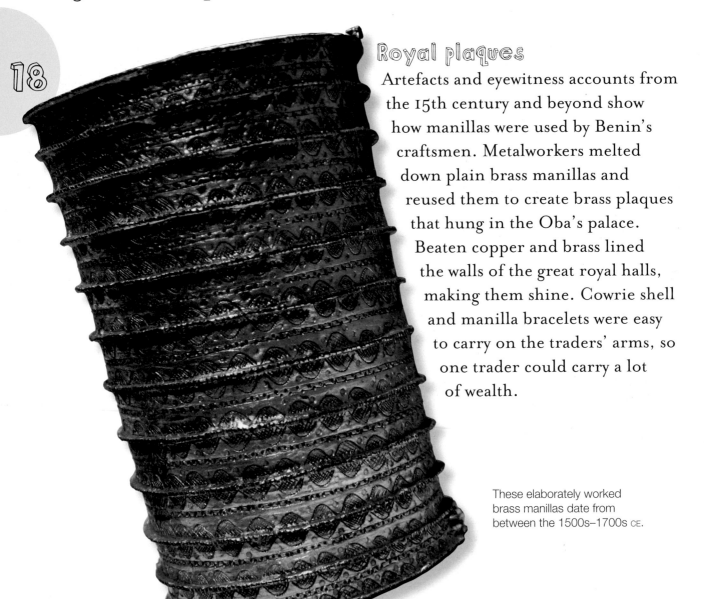

Royal plaques

Artefacts and eyewitness accounts from the 15th century and beyond show how manillas were used by Benin's craftsmen. Metalworkers melted down plain brass manillas and reused them to create brass plaques that hung in the Oba's palace. Beaten copper and brass lined the walls of the great royal halls, making them shine. Cowrie shell and manilla bracelets were easy to carry on the traders' arms, so one trader could carry a lot of wealth.

These elaborately worked brass manillas date from between the 1500s–1700s CE.

From barter to buying

Local markets were set up weekly in the forest region and beyond to barter (exchange goods) rather than pay for them. Later, traders used currencies of cowrie shells and manillas as well as barter. Metalworkers cast the manillas into animal-head sculptures that represented the Oba's mysterious power. From the late 1400s, Portuguese merchants made sure they supplied plenty of good-quality brass manillas to the Edo people.

Cowrie shells were used both as currency and jewellery. Benin oral traditions tell of the second Ogiso, Ere, who wore a crown made of cowries.

19

Kings in control

The Ogiso and Oba controlled all Benin's trade with an iron fist. They took profit from the traders and told them which goods to sell or buy. Trade links stretched across the Sahara to the Mediterranean. From these far-off markets, Benin imported cowrie shells, salt, metals, coral and glass beads. The kings' traders probably met the Saharan traders in markets at the edge of their kingdom.

 ## Around the world

c. 4000–2000 BCE Sumer
Sumerian traders buy goods with gold and silver disks or rings. There are three coins of different values – the shekel, the mina and the talent.

3000 BCE Pakistan/India
In the Indus Valley Civilisation city of Mohenjo-Daro grain is measured on balance scales. Grain is probably bartered for other goods.

900 CE Middle East
Traders buy goods with gold and silver coins. The government officials use glass weights to check the weight of the coins.

WEALTH OF THE FOREST

Benin's forests were full of trees and plants that made elaborate buildings and beautiful craftwork possible. The great halls of the chiefs' houses were supported by sturdy hardwood beams and posts. Builders used wooden scaffolding to reach the curved, conical roofs of these dwellings.

20

Carpenters and carvers

Valuable hardwoods such as black, shiny ebony, red iroko and rich brown mahogany were cut in thick chunks to make the great gateways set into the thick city walls. Or they were carved into sculptures or trinket and gift boxes that belonged to the king. Canoes that transported cargo and soldiers were hollowed out of whole tree trunks. European traders noted that some canoes could carry as many as 80 people.

Cutting edge

Woody, climbing vines called lianas twisted around the great hardwood trees in Benin's forests, often up to 100 metres high. The lianas' stringy fibres were made into rope and twine for tying. They were also handwoven into netting, used for fishing or to carry goods and large pots. Sap or latex were extracted from beneath the bark of some of the forest trees. So Benin's craftsmen had both string and glue to help them hold together their works.

Warriors are shown guarding the highly decorated entrance to the Oba's quarters on this 16th century brass plaque. After the 15th century, the doorposts of the real palace were hung with brass plaques similar to this one, depicting battles and ceremonies.

This pipe-smoking West African man is wearing a hat made of raffia. Raffia is a versatile and valuable material and can be made into many things.

Tough raffia

Raffia is a tough, stringy and waterproof material that comes from the raffia palm, which was readily available in Benin's forests. Benin's craftsmen, and women, used raffia to make cloth, mats, baskets and sturdy frames for shields. Raffia's waterproof quality made it an ideal material for roofing, too.

 ## Around the world

c. 3000-1500 BCE Pakistan/India
The cities of the Indus Valley civilisation have no forests to fuel their kilns, used for firing pottery. Their people cut down every available tree for miles around.

c. 3000–30 BCE Egypt
Reeds are woven into shoes, baskets and even boats, and are used to make papyrus for writing on.

c. 2000 BCE–900 CE Central America
The Maya grow sisal to make rope and cloth.

MUSIC FOR ALL

Music and song entertained the Oba in his palace and the people in their homes and streets. But they were also used to pass traditions from one generation to the next.

Music and power

The musician in the picture on the left is playing a side-blown trumpet in the Oba's court. We can tell he is an important figure by his dress and jewellery. This trumpeter might be playing a fanfare to announce the arrival of the Oba, or to praise him in front of guests. He might also be accompanying oral historians who narrated the deeds of past Ogiso and Oba. This important function of musicians helps us to trace Ogiso, Oba and Benin's people back through time.

This brass figure of a musician dates from between the 1500s–1700s CE.

Studying the evidence

Historians know that when a song and a folktale tell the same story, it is more likely to have actually happened. One song and folktale tell of Ogiso Owodo's only son, Ekaladerhan. He was accused of using magic powers to stop Owodo's wives from having more children. Owodo banished Ekaladerhan and his mother to the forest to die. But Ekaladerhan went on to establish the city of Ughoton.

From bells to drums

Brasses and carved ivories often depict musical instruments, giving us a good idea of their variety and forms. These include bells, drums, flutes, horns, stringed instruments and hand clappers. There are many examples of idiophones, which are carved or cast staves that are struck with a metal rod. Some idiophones are shaped like a drum with a gash in the top. They are also known as slit drums, although they have no membrane (skin) stretched over the top, and so are not true drums.

Who played the music?

Musicians came from guilds. This group of families taught their children to play musical instruments. Some became court musicians, others earnt their living by playing at ceremonies and festivals. These events included age-grade festivals, burials and ceremonies of thanks to the gods and goddesses for a good harvest or other occasion.

23

A court drummer beats two slit drums on this brass plaque dating from the early 1600s.

Around the world

c. 3000–30 BCE Egypt
Musical instruments are played everywhere, from streets to temples. They are often linked to the worship of great gods such as Isis, Sekhmet and Hathor.

c. 2000 BCE–900 CE Central America
Performers entertain rulers and the gods by playing drums, ocarinas, whistles and rattles made from dried gourds.

1600-1050 BCE China
During the Shang Dynasty many musical instruments are played, including the ocarina, stone chimes, panpipes, brass bells and drums, as well as cymbals.

CLEANLINESS AND STYLE

In the 1600s, Dutch visitors wrote that Benin was a city of clean and stylish people. Its inhabitants took pride in their own appearance and in their neat, sparkling homes.

24

Keeping clean

Benin was blessed with plenty of rain and river water for keeping clean. There were pots and jugs for carrying and pouring it. The main picture shows a bronze water jug used by an 18th-century Oba. The water kept his hands clean, especially before taking part in ceremonies. Long ago, we do not know exactly when, the oils of nuts and the cinders of plants were mixed to make very effective soap. It is made to this day.

Style and beauty

Benin's people used wooden combs for their hair. Their skin was decorated with patterned tattoos and scarring. Most people wore beads of blue glass, or red jasper and cornelian stone. The Oba and his chiefs pinned their clothes with large brooches of brass, wood or ivory. These were often fashioned into animal symbols of mystery and power. One of these symbols was the mudfish, which does not seem very exciting. But there is a species of mudfish that can give an electric shock – a powerful image indeed.

This bronze water jug in the shape of a leopard is known as an aquamanile. The tail forms a handle and when the jug is tipped, water pours from the leopard's nostrils.

Cloth for sale in a modern West African market. Most antique cloth was plain but some was striped or chequered. Today's cloth is patterned, as shown here.

Clothworking and clothing

The Edo's famous patterned cloth was exported to other parts of West Africa. Benin's people wore pleated and folded sashes tied around their waists. The sashes were made of local cotton, raffia and bark textiles. The women weavers' looms were upright and could take thick or thin strands. They produced strips of cloth that were sewn together to make larger pieces.

🌐 Around the world

3000-1500 BCE Pakistan/India
In Mohenjo-Daro, people wear beaded jewellery made from lapis lazuli stone, carnelian and agate.

c. 3000–30 BCE Egypt
Egyptians wear linen clothes, made from flax fibres. The flax plant grows along the banks of the River Nile.

c. 2000 BCE–900 CE Central America
Jade jewellery is highly prized by the Maya.

MEDICINE AND MYSTERY

The metal casket below belonged, like most artefacts, to an Oba. This one is probably from the 17th century but it was filled with ancient magic recipes, probably made from forest herbs. The casket and its contents honoured the Oba's ancestors and were a symbol of his enduring power.

26

Cutting edge

Traditional doctors, called Ebo, healed the body, mind and spirit, with the help of Osun, the god of medicine. Ebo understood links between physical and mental health. There were specialists, too, such as the Obodi, who were herbalists, although some medicines were made from birds and animals. Doctors also used divination which means they asked the spirits to help people using mathematics, astrology and ritual objects such as shells or feathers.

The power of potions

The box has a wiggly snake motif as part of the detail on its lid. This is a sure sign of power held within the casket, for this was the same snake symbol that was carved on the roof of the Oba's palace. The Oba was considered an expert in medicine and astrology, which gave him great power. He used his knowledge in ceremonies to please the spirits of past Obas.

The Oba was expected to solve many of his kingdom's problems using medicines and magic recipes held in caskets such as this.

Healing plants

Edo herbalists used stems, bark, roots and leaves of forest plants to make their medicines. They plucked certain species of scented leaves, which helped fevers. They believed that the fruits and leaves of the climbing black pepper, known as Benin pepper, reduced symptoms of sickness, stomach pains, rheumatism and tonsilitis. The *Tetrapleura* pea plant was given to patients suffering from chicken pox, catarrh and high blood pressure.

27

West African markets still sell herbal medicines. Scientists have proved that some herbs offer health benefits and continue to study them.

Around the world

c. 3000–30 BCE Egypt
Egyptian doctors believe that most illnesses are caused by blocked channels in the body. They make medicines to unblock them using spices, clay and animal dung.

c. 2000 BCE–900 CE Central America
The Maya believe that a healthy person needs a balance of the body, spirit and the forces of nature. Healers bleed the body, give herbal medicines and consult the spirits.

900 CE Middle East
Early Islamic science develops, and eventually points the way to some areas of modern medicine. Muhammid ibn Zakariya Razi gains much understanding of allergies and how the eyes work.

THE HEAVEN OF BENIN KINGS

Brass altars were used by the Oba to honour his predecessors. The altar on the right has been elaborately decorated with figures, creatures and plants. Even more important were the rattle staffs, which were, and still are, shaken to show respect to the spirits of the ancestors.

The figure on this plaque holds a rattle staff in the shape of a bamboo rod. All ranks in society used the rattle, which was, for most people, carved from wood.

Gifts and graves

Death traditions go back many centuries. The rituals depended on the clan, gender, age and status of the deceased person. Funerals could take several days and were largely attended by men and women separately. There were musical and theatrical performances from specialist funeral artistes. The dead person was offered gifts and sacrificed goats and fowl, to take with them to heaven. Bodies were often buried in a room or courtyard within the family home

Respecting ancestors

Archaeologists have found ancient courtyards and rooms set aside within Benin homes for honouring ancestral spirits. This was especially true of chiefs and wealthy people. Floors were covered with Benin's traditional paving – ground-down circular pieces of pottery. Set into this tiling were large bottomless pots – their rims level with the surface of the floor. Sacrifices and offerings were ritually placed in the pots, and liquid libations poured over them.

This brass 'altar to the hand', or *ikegobo*, dates from the 1700s–1800s CE and celebrates the deeds of an Oba.

29

Going home

Benin traditions tell of a spiritual homeland for Edo kings to the north, in a city-state called Ile Ife. According to legend, the heads of early Benin kings were taken here for royal ritual burial. According to archaeologists, there is an ancient cemetery in Ile-Ife, *Orun Oba Ado* – meaning the 'heaven of Benin kings'. It contains body parts that could be those of the Ogiso.

Around the world

c. 2000 BCE–900 CE Central America
Rulers are buried in pyramids. The walls of a pyramid tomb in Palenque, Mexico, are painted red. Offerings are placed in the tomb.

1600-1050 BCE China
The Shang believe in the spirits of the ancestors, and their power. Shang kings are buried in vast, decorated tombs together with a lot of other people.

c. 900 BCE Sumer
Sumerians bury food and implements with the dead body. They bury the body in the ground so that the person could be closer to the land of the dead.

GLOSSARY

Adze Cutting tool with a curved blade attached to a handle.

Age grade Age group that has learning targets and social expectations for those within it.

Ancestor Person from whom someone is descended.

Artefact Object that gives clues to the past lives of people who made or owned it.

Artiste A performer.

Barter Exchanging goods rather than paying for them with money.

Brass Metal made from copper and zinc.

Clan Group of families that share the same local history and leader.

Coral Hard rock-like substance made from the skeletons of sea creatures.

Elder Respected senior leader.

Flax A plant grown for its fibres and oil.

Gender Male or female.

Guild An organisation of workers with the same skills.

Hardwood Wood from trees that grow slowly, which makes the wood hard, strong and valuable.

Hereditary Handed down to another member of the same family.

Idiophone A musical instrument that makes a note when struck.

Latex Thick, sticky tree gum.

Mangrove swamp A swamp full of mangrove plants with their twisting stems.

Manilla A thick brass or copper bracelet used as currency.

Merchant Trader of goods.

Moat A deep trench dug around buildings to protect them.

Oral history A spoken or sung history of a people or country.

Ore Rock that contains metal.

Plateau High flat land.

Rampart Flat-topped mound for defending a settlement.

Rattle staff A long staff or stick with hollow rattle at the top.

Ritual Action or actions performed for ceremonial or religious purposes.

Rural In the countryside.

Slave trade The capture and sale of human beings for profit.

Smelt Heating ore to separate the metal it contains from other minerals and impurities.

Staff A long stick.

Yam A large, starchy root that can be eaten.

30

WEBSITES

These websites will give you more information about Benin.

http://www.bbc.co.uk/schools/primaryhistory/worldhistory/benin_bronze/

http://www.britannica.com/EBchecked/topic/60871/Benin

There are some good images of Benin art on this webpage:

http://www.prm.ox.ac.uk/benin.html

See for yourself!
There are museums in the UK, Germany and the USA that hold exhibitions of Benin artefacts. Benin now lies in Nigeria but Nigerian museums have very few exhibits of Edo arts, crafts and royal regalia.

British Museum, London, UK
https://www.britishmuseum.org/

Pitt Rivers Museum, Oxford, UK
http://www.prm.ox.ac.uk/

The Metropolitan Museum of Art,
New York, USA
http://www.metmuseum.org/

The Ethnological Museum of Berlin, Germany
http://www.smb.museum/home.html

Note to parents and teachers
Every effort has been made by the Publishers to ensure that the web sites in this book are suitable for children, that they are of the highest educational value, and that they contain no inappropriate or offensive material. However, because of the nature of the Internet, it is impossible to guarantee that the contents of these sites will not be altered. We strongly advise that Internet access is supervised by a responsible adult.

TIMELINE

4000-2000 BCE The forest site of the Benin Kingdom is occupied by the Edo people.

500-800 CE The Edo practise successful agriculture and trade. Villages grow and are led by a chief, who is the oldest man in the village.

800-900 CE It is thought that the first Ogiso king, Ogiso Igodo, rules over all Edo villages. The kingdom is called Igodomigodo and the Ogiso rules with the advice of the Uzama.

800-1255 CE Trade expands within West Africa and beyond. Goods come across the Sahara from as far as the Mediterranean. Brass, ivory, cloth, beadwork and other fine crafts develop.

1255 CE The Uzama becomes too quarrelsome. Oba Ewedo takes over from the Ogiso kings and curbs the Uzama's power. The title, Oba, replaces Ogiso.

1255-1400s CE The Kingdom of Benin expands outside the city.

1480s-1600s CE Portuguese and Dutch traders visit Benin and strike up trade deals. Oba expand their power and empire through controlling trade in black pepper, palm oil, animal skins, ivory and slaves.

1600s-1800s Benin City declines slowly as other states around it grow stronger.

1896-7 The Oba suspects that the British want to take over his territory, so he shuts them out. A British force invades, raids and loots Benin. Colonial rule begins.

Today Benin lies in Edo State, Nigeria. Its people still keep many ancient traditions, including an Oba in his palace.

INDEX

32